EARTH-FRIENDLY ANIMAL CRAFTS

Veronica Thompson

Lerner Publications ◆ Minneapolis

Lerner Publications Company
A division of Lerner Publishing Group, Inc.
241 First Avenue North
Minneapolis, MN 55401 USA

For reading levels and more information, look up this title at www.lernerbooks.com.

Main body text set in Avenir LT Pro 12/16.
Typeface provided by Linotype AG.

Photo Acknowledgments
The images in this book are used with the permission of: © cosmaa/Shutterstock Images, p. 1 (Earth icon); © Stilesta/Shutterstock Images, pp. 1, 3, 9, 11, 13, 15, 17, 19, 21, 23, 25, 27, 28 (border design element); © Africa Studio/Shutterstock Images, p. 4 (boy and dog); © Coltty/Shutterstock Images, p. 4 (cow); © chuchiko17/Shutterstock Images, p. 5; © Javier Somoza/Shutterstock Images, p. 6 (jar); © urfin/Shutterstock Images, p. 6 (clothes); © xpixel/Shutterstock Images, p. 6 (towel); © Joanna Dorota/Shutterstock Images, p. 7; Veronica Thompson, pp. 8, 9 (top), 9 (center), 9 (bottom left), 9 (bottom right), 10, 11 (top), 11 (center), 11 (bottom), 12, 13 (top), 13 (center), 13 (bottom), 14, 15 (top), 15 (center), 15 (bottom), 16, 17 (top), 17 (center), 17 (bottom), 18, 19 (top), 19 (center), 19 (bottom), 20, 21 (top), 21 (center), 21 (bottom), 22, 23 (top), 23 (center), 23 (bottom), 24, 25 (top), 25 (center), 25 (bottom), 26, 27 (top), 27 (center), 27 (bottom), 28 (top), 28 (center), 28 (bottom); © Curly Pat/Shutterstock Images, pp. 9, 11, 13, 15, 17, 19, 21, 23, 25, 27, 28 (design element); © Dawna Moore/Shutterstock Images, p. 29 (top); © Hong Vo/Shutterstock Images, p. 29 (bottom); © FlashMovie/Shutterstock Images, p. 30; © ifong/Shutterstock Images, p. 31; © Daria Rybakova/Shutterstock Images, p. 32 (top); Courtesy Veronica Thompson, p. 32 (bottom)

Front cover: Veronica Thompson (main); © cosmaa/Shutterstock Images (Earth icon)
Back cover: © Curly Pat/Shutterstock Images (background design element); © Stilesta/Shutterstock Images (border design element)

Library of Congress Cataloging-in-Publication Data

The Cataloging-in-Publication Data for *Earth-Friendly Animal Crafts* is on file at the Library of Congress.
978-1-5415-2421-7 (lib. bdg.)
978-1-5415-2778-2 (pbk.)
978-1-5415-2427-9 (eb pdf)

Manufactured in the United States of America
1-44515-34765-4/30/2018

CONTENTS

Animals ~ 4

The Basics ~ ~ ~ ~ ~ ~ ~ ~ ~ ~ ~ ~ ~ ~ ~ ~ ~ ~ 6

Roaring Wall Art ~ ~ ~ ~ ~ ~ ~ ~ ~ ~ ~ ~ ~ ~ 8

T-Shirt Dog Toy ~ ~ ~ ~ ~ ~ ~ ~ ~ ~ ~ ~ ~ ~ 10

Bee Seed Bombs ~ ~ ~ ~ ~ ~ ~ ~ ~ ~ ~ ~ ~ ~ 12

Cozy Cap Owl Pillow ~ ~ ~ ~ ~ ~ ~ ~ ~ ~ ~ 14

Frog Koozie ~ ~ ~ ~ ~ ~ ~ ~ ~ ~ ~ ~ ~ ~ ~ ~ ~ 16

Retro Diner Bird Feeder ~ ~ ~ ~ ~ ~ ~ 18

Animal Night-Light ~ ~ ~ ~ ~ ~ ~ ~ ~ ~ ~ 20

Towel Pet Bed ~ ~ ~ ~ ~ ~ ~ ~ ~ ~ ~ ~ ~ ~ ~ 22

Fox Lunch Bag ~ ~ ~ ~ ~ ~ ~ ~ ~ ~ ~ ~ ~ ~ ~ 24

Bear Book Cover ~ ~ ~ ~ ~ ~ ~ ~ ~ ~ ~ ~ ~ 26

Odds & Ends ~ ~ ~ ~ ~ ~ ~ ~ ~ ~ ~ ~ ~ ~ ~ ~ ~ 29

Glossary ~ ~ ~ ~ ~ ~ ~ ~ ~ ~ ~ ~ ~ ~ ~ ~ ~ ~ ~ 30

Further Information ~ ~ ~ ~ ~ ~ ~ ~ ~ ~ 31

Index ~ 32

Scan QR codes throughout for
step-by-step pictures of each craft.

ANIMALS

Recycling and reusing products can help keep trash from ending up in animal habitats. It can also reduce the number of resources, such as trees, used to make products for humans.

Get ready to repurpose items to make cool crafts for and featuring animals!

CHOOSING MATERIALS

When you're gathering things to repurpose, ask for permission before cutting up old clothing items or towels. Also ask an adult before reusing something that isn't in the recycling bin. The item may be serving another purpose already!

CLEAN MACHINE

Reused materials may carry germs, dirt, or leftover food. Give these materials a good scrub before crafting with them! Wash and dry old T-shirts and towels. Rinse out recycled jars. And wipe down an old lunch bag before using it for a craft.

STAY SAFE!

Some crafts in this book require sharp or hot tools. Ask for an adult's help when using these items:
- craft knife
- hot glue gun

ROARING WALL ART

Make a wild animal for your wall! Repurpose recycled paper products into a colorful lion mane.

MATERIALS
- cardboard
- scissors
- old magazines and newspapers
- paper grocery bags
- tape
- crayons, colored pencils, or markers
- string

STEM Takeaway
Only male lions have manes. One purpose of the mane is to attract female lions.

1 Cut a large cardboard circle.

2 Cut magazine and newspaper pages and a paper grocery bag into thin strips.

3 Bend one strip in half and tape its ends near the edge of the cardboard circle. Repeat around the **perimeter** of the circle.

4 Repeat step 2 to make more rows of looped paper. Tape each row a bit nearer the center of the cardboard.

5 Cut a lion face from another paper grocery bag. Draw or color the lion's facial features on it. Then tape the face to the center of the cardboard.

6 Tape a loop of string to the back of the lion. Use it to hang up your wild work of art!!

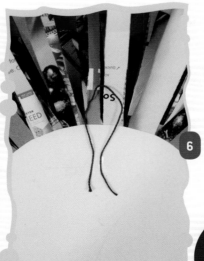

Scan the QR code for more photos.

T-SHIRT DOG TOY

Cut and braid old T-shirts to turn them into a tennis-ball tug rope!

MATERIALS
~ two old T-shirts
~ scissors
~ ruler
~ old tennis ball
~ craft knife

1 Cut the shirts into nine long strips, each 2 inches (5 cm) wide. Knot the strips together at one end.

2 Braid the strips in groups of three. Knot the ends of all the braided strips together.

3 Have an adult use a craft knife to cut a 1-inch (2.5 cm) slit in the tennis ball. Do not make the slit larger. Its small size keeps the strip's knot from slipping out later.

4 Have an adult squeeze the tennis ball hard to open the slit. Push the knot into the slit. The slit will close tight around the knot when the ball is let go. Your toy is now ready for play time with your pup!

SWAP IT!
Swap T-shirts for old towels or blankets.

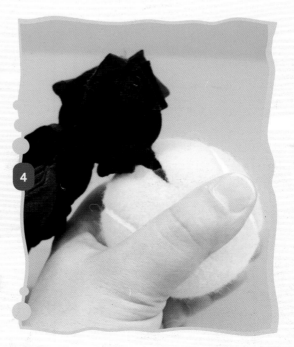

BEE SEED BOMBS

Use leftover bits of soil and seeds to make seed bombs that will grow bee-friendly flowers!

MATERIALS
- ~ measuring cups
- ~ clay flour
- ~ leftover potting soil
- ~ leftover bee-friendly seeds, such as lavender, rosemary, sage, catnip, oregano, black-eyed Susan, and verbena
- ~ water
- ~ bowl
- ~ baking sheet
- ~ aluminum foil
- ~ cookie cutters

STEM Takeaway
Bee-friendly flowers produce lots of nectar that bees can eat. Their shapes make it easy for bees to collect pollen.

1 Add 1 cup clay flour, 1⅔ cup soil, ⅓ cup seeds, and ⅔ cup water to the bowl.

2 Mix the ingredients with your hands.

3 Set the cookie cutters on a baking sheet lined with foil. Fill each cookie cutter with the soil mixture.

4 Place the sheet in a sunny spot and allow the soil mix to dry for twenty-four hours. If you're in a cloudy area, allow the mix to dry near a window for three days.

5 Carefully push the dry seed bombs from the cookie cutters.

6 Place the seed bombs into a garden or planter. No need to bury them. Just water the seed bombs once a week. Then wait and watch for them to sprout!

SWAP IT!
Swap clay flour for clay. Mix 5 parts clay, 1 part soil, and 1 part seeds. Sprinkle in a little water.

COZY CAP OWL PILLOW

Turn an old knit beanie into a tiny stuffed owl!

MATERIALS

- ribbon
- measuring tape or ruler
- scissors
- old knit beanie
- crochet hook
- bobby pin or safety pin
- cotton stuffing
- recycled felt or fabric scraps
- hot glue gun & glue sticks, or fabric glue

1 Cut a piece of ribbon 18 inches (46 cm) long.

2 If the beanie has a folded rim, unfold it. A few inches above the rim, poke a crochet hook through from inside the hat. Loop one end of the ribbon around the hook, then pull all but a few inches of the ribbon inside the hat. Keep the ribbon tail in place outside the hat using a bobby pin or safety pin.

3 Use the hook to weave the ribbon in and out of the hat around its perimeter. Keep the ribbon end in place using the same pin from step 2.

4 Fill the hat with cotton stuffing! Then remove the pin and pull the ribbon ends like a **drawstring**. Pull the hat nearly closed, but leave a small opening. Knot the ribbon ends and push the extra hat rim fabric inside the pillow through the small hole.

5 Shape the pillow into a thick disc and flip it so the ribbon faces down.

SWAP IT!

Swap the cotton stuffing for cut-up pieces of old T-shirts or socks.

6 Cut an owl face, beak, and eyes from felt or fabric scraps. Glue them to the pillow. If you want your owl to wear a bow, use the crochet hook to thread some ribbon through the top of the pillow. Then tie it in a bow!

FROG KOOZIE

Reuse a recycled glass container again and again as a water bottle! Make a cozy frog koozie to keep the bottle safe.

STEM Takeaway
There are about 4,740 frog species in the world! Frogs live on every continent but Antarctica.

MATERIALS
- recycled glass bottle with cap
- water
- dish soap
- 8.5" x 11" felt sheet in green
- binder clips
- hot glue gun & glue sticks, or fabric glue
- scissors
- felt or fabric scraps in various colors

OPTIONAL
- small plastic tub

1 Remove any paper labels from the bottle. Fill a sink or small plastic tub with warm, soapy water and soak the bottle for one hour. Remove the bottle and peel the labels off.

2 Set the dry bottle in the center of a sheet of felt. Pull up the short sides of the felt so they meet on either side of the bottle. Fold extra felt on the right side and clip it snugly to the bottle.

3 Remove the bottle. Turn the felt inside out.

4 Apply a line of glue along the line created by the clips. Turn the felt right side out again and press down where the glue is.

5 Fit the felt around the bottle again, then fold and clip the other open side and repeat step 3. When the glue dries, turn the koozie inside out and trim any extra felt from the sides. Then turn the koozie right side out again.

6 Cut along the opening of the koozie to make two arcs near the front center. These will hold the frog's eyes.

7 Cut eyes, **nostrils**, skin patterns, and other frog features from felt. Glue them to the koozie. When the glue dries, your frog is ready to **ferry** your new water bottle!

RETRO DINER BIRD FEEDER

Convert a recycled jar and a plastic plate into a bird feeder that looks like a retro diner!

MATERIALS
- ~ recycled canning jar with lid
- ~ paint
- ~ paint brushes
- ~ birdseed
- ~ 4 medium beads of the same size
- ~ hot glue gun & glue sticks
- ~ plastic plate

1 Remove the lid from the jar. Recycle the lid disc and keep the ring. Turn the jar upside down and paint it in a bright color to look like a diner. Leave some areas free of paint as windows.

2 Make up a diner name and paint it on the jar. Paint a line to remind you when to fill the feeder.

3 Once the paint dries, set the jar upright and fill it with birdseed.

4 Glue the beads to the top of the metal lid ring, spaced evenly apart. Let the glue dry.

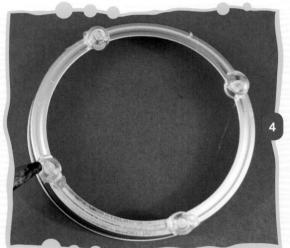

5 Place more hot glue on top of each bead. Then quickly and carefully flip the ring onto the plate. Let the glue dry.

6 Flip the plate over and set the lid on the jar. Place your hand flat in the center of the plate and turn it to screw the lid onto the jar. When the lid is on, quickly flip the entire feeder over so it sits on the plate. Set the feeder up outside and watch birds flock to the diner for food!

7 To refill your feeder, flip it upside down and place your hand flat in the center of the plate. Turn the plate to unscrew the lid. Then fill the jar with more birdseed and repeat step 6.

ANIMAL NIGHT-LIGHT

Turn used tissue paper and a recycled jar into a bright animal bedside light!

MATERIALS
~ recycled glass jar
~ recycled tissue paper
~ scissors
~ craft glue
~ paint brush or foam brush
~ battery-powered candle

1 Flatten the tissue paper. Then plan your design! Cut one large piece of tissue as the animal face. Measure to make sure the face is not taller than the jar.

2 Cut features from tissue paper. This includes eyes, ears, a nose, and mouth. It could also include **whiskers** or teeth. Assemble the animal face before gluing.

3 Brush glue onto the jar and attach the animal face.

4 Cut other colors of tissue paper into small shapes. Brush glue onto the exposed jar and cover it in the shapes.

5 Let the glue dry. Then place a battery-operated candle inside the jar. Watch your animal come to life with light!

SWAP IT!
Use battery-powered string lights if you don't have a battery-powered candle.

TOWEL PET BED

Give old towels new purpose as a comfy bed for your indoor pets!

MATERIALS
- ~ old towels
- ~ scissors
- ~ ruler
- ~ crochet hook
- ~ yarn
- ~ cotton stuffing

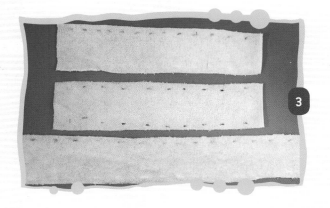

1 To make a small bed, use one towel. Fold it into thirds and cut along the last fold to remove one third. Set the third aside and fold the larger piece in half.

To make a larger bed, use two towels. Fold one in half.

2 Along every top edge but the folded one, cut small slits. Make each slit 1 inch (2.5 cm) apart, and about 1 inch (2.5 cm) from the towel edge. Cut matching slits along all bottom edges but the folded one.

3 Cut the extra third or extra towel from step 1 or 2 into three pieces. Make one the length of the long side of the folded towel. Make two pieces the length of the short side of the folded towel. These will be the bed side pieces. Cut slits 1 inch (2.5 cm) apart along each piece's long edges.

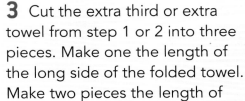

4 Use the crochet hook and yarn to stitch the two long side pieces to the top and bottom of the pet bed.

5 Fill the bed with stuffing. Then repeat step 5 on the short side. Your Earth-friendly craft is ready for your pet!

SWAP IT!

Swap the towels for old blankets and the cotton stuffing for old T-shirts.

FOX LUNCH BAG

Use fabric scraps to revamp an old lunch bag to look like a fox!

MATERIALS
~ fabric lunch bag
~ fabric glue
~ leftover fabric or felt scraps
~ scissors

STEM Takeaway
A female fox is called a vixen.
A male is called a dog fox!

1 Patch any holes or tears in the lunch bag using fabric glue. As you plan your fox face, aim to cover these areas with fabric if you can.

2 Cut shapes from fabric scraps to make fox eyes, ears, nose, and mouth.

3 Assemble the shapes from step 2 and glue any layers together for the eyes and ears.

4 Glue the features from step 3 to the lunch bag. Allow the glue to dry.

5 If any pieces hang over the edge of the lunch bag or are in the way of the zipper, trim them. Your fox lunch bag is ready to be filled!

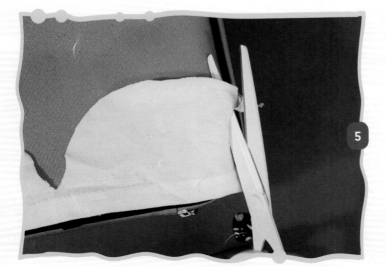

SWAP IT!

Swap the lunch bag for an old backpack! Repair any tears or holes. Then glue on fabric features to make an animal face.

BEAR BOOK COVER

Protect a book with a cut-up old sweatshirt made to look like a bear!

MATERIALS
- old sweatshirt
- scissors
- book
- ruler
- chalk
- hot glue gun & glue sticks or fabric glue
- binder clips
- recycled felt and fabric scraps

STEM Takeaway

Three bear species live in North America. They are the black bear, brown bear, and polar bear.

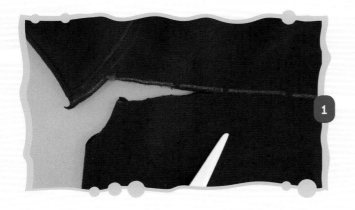

1 Cut a **horizontal** line through the sweatshirt just under the arms. Set the top piece aside.

2 Lay the closed book on top of the sweatshirt, near its left edge. Measure 3 inches (7.6 cm) from the right of the book and draw a line in chalk. Cut the line and set the extra material aside.

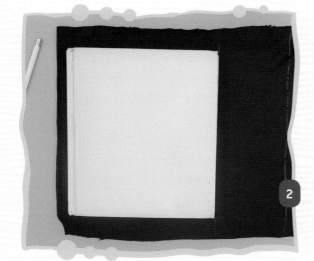

3 Remove the book and unfold the sweatshirt. Set the open book in the center of the sweatshirt. Press the covers flat and draw a horizontal and vertical line from each corner to the edge of the fabric. Draw two vertical lines at the top and bottom of the book's spine to the fabric edge. Cut along all lines to remove six rectangles of fabric. This creates flaps.

Bear Book Cover continued on next page

4 Fold the flaps over the back cover and glue them together at the corners. Do not glue the fabric to the book. Hold the corners together with binder clips as the glue dries. Repeat this step for the front cover.

5 Cut two strips of fabric from the extra sweatshirt material. Make each strip as long as the book is tall. Glue the ends of one piece to the top and bottom flap at the back cover, near the spine. Use binder clips to hold the piece in place while the glue dries. Repeat this step with the second strip on the front cover.

6 Cut a nose, mouth, eyes, and ears from the extra sweatshirt and fabric scraps. Glue these features to the front cover to make a bear face!

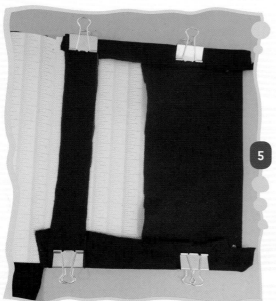

ODDS & ENDS

Craft materials and a little creativity can give new life to all kinds of old or recycled materials. What else can you repurpose?

SUNGLASSES

Pop the lenses out of old sunglasses. Attach paper animal ears and noses to make a fun photo prop!

SEASHELLS

Repurpose old seashells into little pets! Make a crab or snail body out of clay and stuff it in the shell. Then glue on googly eyes.

SOCKS

Put a tennis ball in an old sock and tie a knot to keep it in place. This makes a great dog toy!

HEADBANDS

Cover damaged headbands in colorful duct tape. Form animal ears from the tape too. You could make cat, dog, fox, bear, or even elephant ears!

T-SHIRT

Cut an old T-shirt into short strips. Stack the strips and tie them around the middle with a long string. This turns the strips into a pom-pom. Hold the string and shake the pom-pom as a toy for your cat!

MAGAZINES

Cut animal images out of magazines and glue them to cardboard to make animal puppets! You can also place the cardboard animals in old shoeboxes decorated to look like the animals' habitat.

GLOSSARY

attract: to draw the interest of someone or something

creativity: the use of the imagination to think of new ideas

drawstring: a string that closes or tightens a bag or piece of clothing when you pull the ends

ferry: to carry things from one place to another

habitats: the natural environments of a person, plant, or animal

horizontal: straight and level, parallel to the ground

koozie: a fabric or foam sleeve used to keep a drink cold

nostrils: the two openings in the nose that an animal breathes and smells through

perimeter: the distance around the outside edge of an area or shape

repurpose: to give a new purpose or use

resources: things that are of value or use

retro: style that copies the fashion or design from the recent past

revamp: to remake or redesign

species: one of the groups into which animals and plants are divided

whiskers: the long, stiff hairs near the mouths of some animals

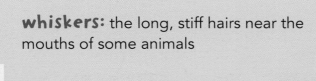

FURTHER INFORMATION

BOOKS

Bernhardt, Carolyn. *Duct Tape Animals.*
Minneapolis: Lerner Publications, 2017.
Find tons of ideas to turn tape into cool animal crafts, such as a mounted moose head and a bright snake!

Bosch, Sammy. *Super Simple Backyard Critter Crafts: Fun and Easy Animal Crafts.* Minneapolis: Super Sandcastle/Abdo Publishing, 2017.
Create fun and easy animal crafts and learn about backyard animal habitats!

Radford, Tracey. *Make Your Own Zoo: 35 Projects for Kids Using Everyday Cardboard Packaging.*
London: CICO Books, 2015.
Learn to turn cardboard into zoo animals! Make zebras, crocodiles, penguins, parrots, and more. Instructions for creating cardboard animal habitats are also included.

WEBSITES

Free Kids Crafts: Pet Crafts for Kids
http://www.freekidscrafts.com/animal -crafts-for-kids/pet-crafts-for-kids/
Free printable instructions to make crafts for and featuring your favorite pets!

I Heart Crafty Things: 50+ Zoo Animal Crafts for Kids
https://iheartcraftythings.com/50-zoo -animal-crafts-kids.html
Check out these links to all kinds of simple crafts featuring zoo animals.

PBS: Crafts for Kids—All Animal Crafts
http://www.pbs.org/parents/crafts-for -kids/category/type-and-medium/animal -crafts/
Browse dozens of animal crafts you can make with household and recycled items.

INDEX

animal night-light, 20–21

bear book cover, 26–28
bears, 26, 28, 29
bees, 12
bee seed bombs, 12–13
bird feeder, 18–19

flowers, 12
foxes, 24–25, 29
fox lunch bag, 24–25
frog koozie, 16–17
frogs, 16–17

habitats, 4, 29

lions, 8–9
lion wall art, 8–9

materials, 6–7, 8, 10, 12,
    14, 16, 18, 20, 22, 24,
    26, 29

owl pillow, 14–15

pet crafts, 10–11, 22–23

recycling, 4, 6, 8, 16,
    18–19, 20, 29
resources, 4

safety, 7

towel pet bed, 22–23
T-shirt dog toy, 10–11

ABOUT THE AUTHOR/ PHOTOGRAPHER

Veronica Thompson lives in a little brownstone in Brooklyn, New York, with her two puppies and wonderful husband. She spends her days crafting for her website, makescoutdiy.com, and building websites.